Snowy Owls
Whoo Are They?

W9-AVI-200

Ansley Watson Ford and Denver W. Holt

Illustrated by Jennifer White Bohman

2008
Mountain Press Publishing Company
Missoula, Montana

Text © 2008 by Ansley Watson Ford and Denver W. Holt
Illustrations © 2008 by Jennifer White Bohman

Photographs © Daniel J. Cox/NaturalExposures.com

Library of Congress Cataloging-in-Publication Data

Ford, Ansley Watson, 1975–
   Snowy owls : whoo are they? / Ansley Watson Ford and Denver W. Holt ; illustrated by Jennifer White Bohman.
     p. cm.
   ISBN 978-0-87842-543-3 (pbk. : alk. paper)
   1. Snowy owl—Juvenile literature. I. Holt, D. W. (Denver W.) II. Bohman, Jennifer, ill.
III. Title.
  QL696.S83F67 2008
  598.9'7—dc22

2008000059

Printed in Hong Kong by Mantec Production Company

Mountain Press Publishing Company
P.O. Box 2399, Missoula, MT 59806
406-728-1900

Dedicated to all of us, young and old, who find joy
and inspiration in the wonders of nature. —AWF

To the people of Barrow, Alaska, and especially to the Native Iñupiats for allowing me to
conduct research on their land, and to the many friends I've made in Barrow. —DWH

My work in this book is dedicated to my husband, John, for his constant support, and to my
son, Reuben, who waited patiently until days after my paintings were finished to be born.
—JWB

 HOO . . . is big and white and feathered all over? Whoo is a strong, skillful hunter, flying thousands of miles in search of the best meal? Whoo spends time perched on the shoulder of the famous wizard Harry Potter? The answer to all of these questions is . . . you guessed it, the Snowy Owl! What makes this large, white bird so special? Let's head to the snow-covered north to find out.

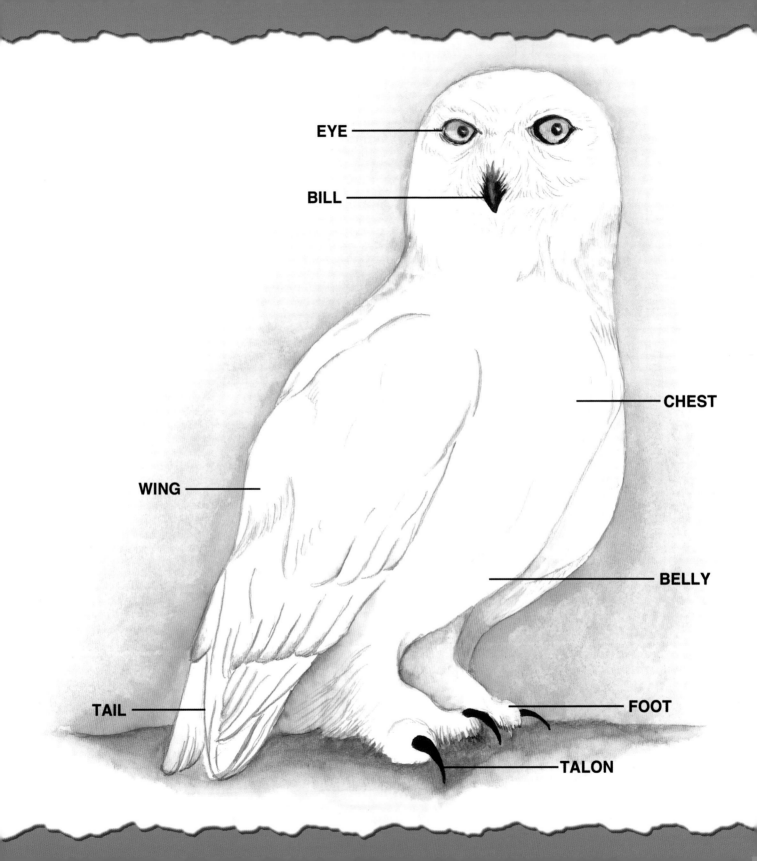

EYE

BILL

CHEST

WING

BELLY

TAIL

FOOT

TALON

North to the Arctic

Have you ever been to the Arctic? Not many people have. The Arctic is the northernmost part of the Earth, above an imaginary line called the **Arctic Circle**. In the middle of that circle is the North Pole. North of the Arctic Circle you'll find a unique kind of landscape called **tundra**. Tundra is mostly treeless terrain that is found high in the mountains (**alpine tundra**) or very far north (**Arctic tundra**). In these places cold weather and short growing seasons mean that only plants like grasses, mosses, lichens, and low shrubs can grow. Which kind of tundra will be the setting for this book? If you guessed *Arctic* tundra, you're correct.

The Arctic tundra can be a very cold place, and only specially **adapted** plants and animals can live there. **Adaptations** are characteristics that give living things their best chance at survival. What kind of adaptations might an animal need to have in order to survive very cold weather? Thick fur? Feathered feet? Winter migration? Hibernation? These are all ways that certain animals have adapted to living in cold, snowy places.

GLOBE TROTTER!
Grab a globe and locate the Arctic Circle. Snowy Owls are **circumpolar**, which means they can be found anywhere within the circle around the North Pole (during the summer months). Can you name all of the countries that have land above the Arctic Circle?

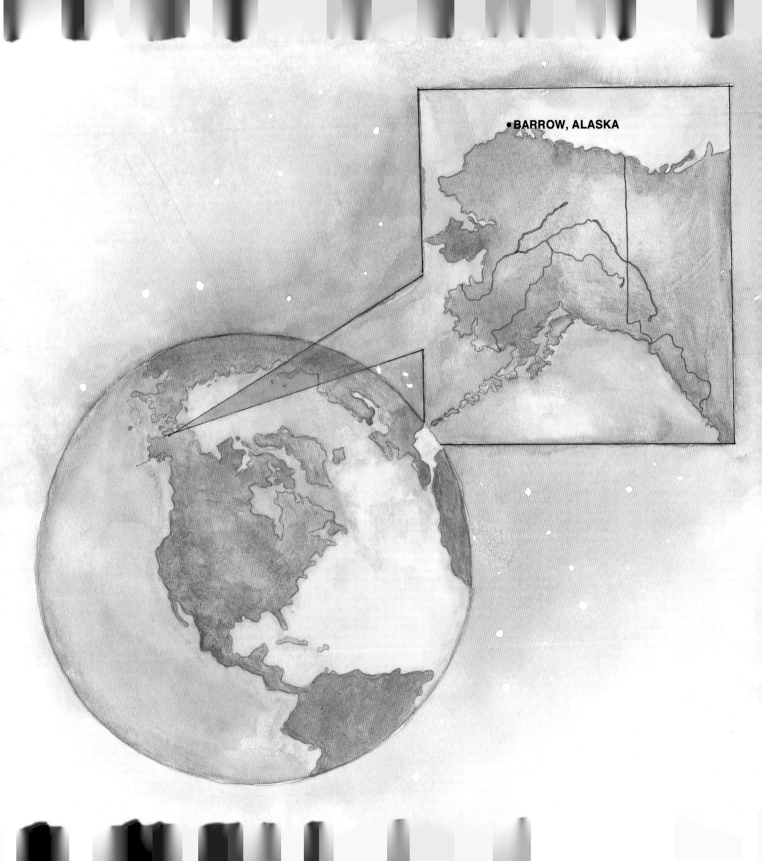

BARROW, ALASKA

Hardy Humans

People can adapt to living in very cold climates too. The village of **Barrow, Alaska**, on the coast of the Arctic Ocean is farther north than any other town in the United States. If you were exploring the Arctic around Barrow you would meet a group of people called the **Iñupiat** (pronounced in-new-pea-ot). The Iñupiat people have lived in the Arctic for thousands of years among Polar Bears, caribou, Arctic Foxes, and an enormous bird scientists call *Bubo scandiacus*, better known as the **Snowy Owl**.

The Iñupiat people of Barrow have a long history with the Snowy Owl. In their native language of **Iñupiaq** (in-new-pea-ock), Snowy Owls are called **Ukpik** (pronounced ook-pik). The land of and around Barrow was originally named **Ukpeaǧvik** (ook-pee-og-vik), which means "place where Snowy Owls are hunted." Snowy Owls and their eggs were traditionally used as a food source for the Iñupiat people.

Throughout history, owls have been thought of as "mystical" or even "magical" by people of many different cultures. These days one Snowy Owl is well known as the companion to a young boy with magical powers. That's right—much of the Snowy Owl's recent fame can be credited to Hedwig, the Snowy Owl belonging to Harry Potter in the famous book series. Why do you think this large white bird might be seen as magical by some people?

Handy Hunters

Like eagles, ospreys, hawks, and falcons, Snowy Owls are **raptors** or **birds of prey**. Birds of prey are **predators** (hunters), hunting for live **prey** (food) to eat. Their prey can be insects, fish, amphibians, reptiles, small mammals, and even other birds! Like other raptors, owls have special features that make them great hunters, such as strong beaks and sharp **talons**, or claws. Owls, however, do not look and act the same as other birds of prey. Owls are easily recognized by their large, round heads, flat faces, forward-facing eyes, and fluffy-looking bodies.

Ukpik has big, thickly feathered feet to keep warm and sharp talons to grasp prey. Its black beak is nearly hidden by long, white facial feathers but is sharp and strong to grip and tear prey. With their keen vision, the Snowy Owl's catlike yellow eyes make it possible to spot prey as small as a mouse from over 300 feet away. That's the length of a football field!

Many owls are **nocturnal**, meaning they are active at night. Other owls are **diurnal**, hunting during the day. During the Arctic summer the sun does not set in Barrow for about twelve weeks, so the Snowy Owl can't help but be mainly diurnal during the breeding season; it is mostly nocturnal the rest of the year but may hunt day or night. Sounds like Snowies really like to hunt! In the Alaskan Arctic near Barrow, Ukpik hunts mostly **Brown Lemmings**, the small mouselike creatures of the tundra, and also weasels and many types of birds.

Why Be White?

If you ever happen to be trudging across the Arctic tundra of Alaska and an enormous white bird crosses your path, you can be pretty sure you've seen a Snowy Owl. The Snowy Owl is the heaviest North American owl and one of the largest birds of prey in the Arctic, second only to eagles. A Snowy Owl weighs only 5 pounds at the most, but that's a lot for a bird. Ukpik stands 21 to 26 inches tall and has a **wingspan** of over 5 feet. Imagine lying down next to a Snowy Owl. Its outstretched wings could be longer than your entire body!

More striking than its size is the brilliant, pure white color of the male Snowy Owl's feathers. Why be white? Many animals are the color of their surroundings. This is called **camouflage**, which is an animal's way of being less visible to predators and prey. Some Arctic animals are white to blend in with ice and snow. But what happens when summer comes? Many animals, like the Snowshoe Hare and Willow Ptarmigan, change into summertime fur or feathers of brown. But not the Snowy Owl! It remains a white beacon even in summer. Why? Scientists aren't sure. Perhaps it's because the Arctic summer is so short (sometimes fewer than two snow-free months) that there isn't time to grow a new set of feathers. Why change when you spend most of your life surrounded by snow?

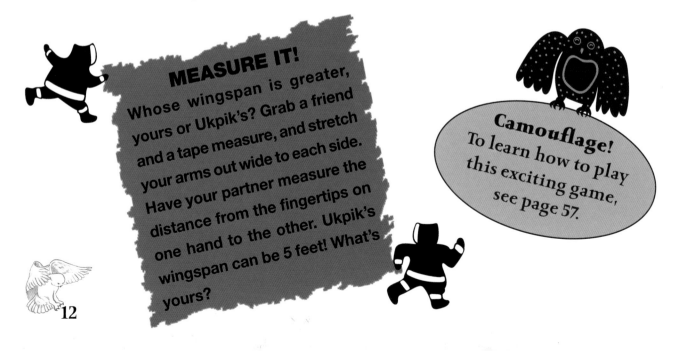

MEASURE IT!

Whose wingspan is greater, yours or Ukpik's? Grab a friend and a tape measure, and stretch your arms out wide to each side. Have your partner measure the distance from the fingertips on one hand to the other. Ukpik's wingspan can be 5 feet! What's yours?

Camouflage!
To learn how to play this exciting game, see page 57.

Why Be Different?

In many birds it is easy to tell the male and female apart. Often the male is brightly colored, which helps him attract a mate. In most owl species, however, the male and female look quite similar. Not so with the Snowy! Like many other predatory birds, female Snowy Owls are significantly larger than males, averaging about 25 inches in body length, compared to the male's 23 inches. Females weigh about 4½ to 5 pounds, while the males are 3 to 4 pounds. In many animals, including people, the male is often larger. Why do you think female Snowy Owls would outsize their mates? Scientists think females have larger bodies to store more fat for motherhood. Mother owls need to keep the eggs warm in their cold environment, and a larger body retains more heat. Those fat reserves also come in handy while she stays on the nest waiting for the male to bring her food.

When deciding whether a Snowy Owl is male or female, comparing body size is tricky unless a pair is roosted together. Easier to spot are the dark bars or dots on the female, in contrast to the male's pure white feathers. It can be easy to confuse an adult female with a young Snowy Owl, but young owls have more dark spotting than their mother. Can you guess why the young might be colored this way? If you guessed camouflage again, you're probably right! The mottled white and black feathers may help young owls blend in with their summer surroundings and hide from predators like Arctic Foxes.

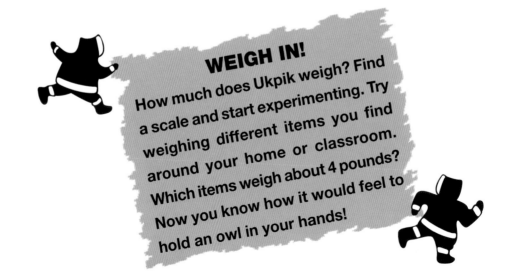

WEIGH IN!

How much does Ukpik weigh? Find a scale and start experimenting. Try weighing different items you find around your home or classroom. Which items weigh about 4 pounds? Now you know how it would feel to hold an owl in your hands!

Finding a Mate

Birds nesting means springtime and flowers, right? Not for Snowy Owls! When they return to their Arctic coastal **breeding grounds** to look for a mate in late April or May, the tundra is still frozen and snow covered! During the month of May, male Snowy Owls are busy establishing and defending their territories against other males. When two male Snowies disagree on territorial boundaries, they stand facing each other, bow forward, and hoot back and forth. That would get your attention, wouldn't it?

The hooting also gets the attention of female owls. When a male spots a female he wants to mate with, he tries to win her over with a **courtship flight**, flying in an exaggerated undulating pattern. To **undulate** means to move up and down like waves. If you drew a line showing the courtship flight pattern it would look like a wavy line moving across the sky. Ukpik flies high, holding his wings in a V shape above his body. As he does this, he loses altitude, dropping down lower and lower. Then with rapid wing strokes he quickly regains altitude and repeats the process.

After the courtship flight, the male might land and offer the female a lemming. He presents it to her, waiting for the female's response. Sometimes the female accepts the lemming right away. Other times, the male has to repeat his offer several times before the pair decides to mate.

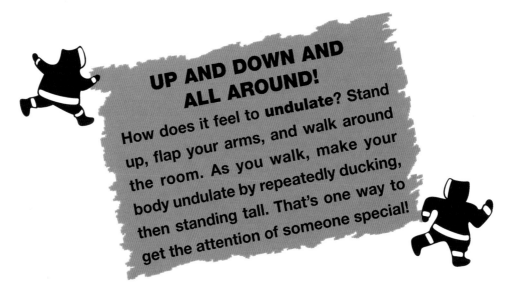

UP AND DOWN AND ALL AROUND!

How does it feel to **undulate**? Stand up, flap your arms, and walk around the room. As you walk, make your body undulate by repeatedly ducking, then standing tall. That's one way to get the attention of someone special!

16

To Nest or Not to Nest

Most birds **nest** every year, finding a mate, choosing a nest site, and raising a family. Some even nest three or four times a year! We have learned that Snowy Owls are different from other birds in many ways. Do you think that they nest every year? If you guessed no, you're right!

Scientists think that Snowy Owls nest only during those summers when food is abundant. Brown Lemmings, the key food source of the Snowy Owls around Barrow, have population levels that **fluctuate** widely. This means that their numbers will be very large and very small in other years. Many animals have fluctuating populations. When an area has a small population of a certain species there can be more food available for each individual, so the animals are healthy and reproduce more frequently. Their population begins to grow, and soon they are no longer small in numbers. Once the population is larger, there is not as much food available to each individual, some will not survive, and the population becomes smaller again. This fluctuation is called a **population cycle**.

What does the lemming population cycle have to do with Snowy Owls? Well, if the lemming population is low, owls may not be able to find enough food to feed themselves *and* a nest of hungry chicks. They may wait for a nesting season when the lemming population is on the rise so they can raise many fat, healthy chicks.

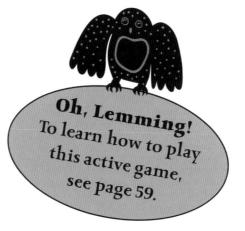

Oh, Lemming! To learn how to play this active game, see page 59.

18

Nesting Neighborhood

All parents want to raise their children in a safe neighborhood, and so do Snowy Owl parents. Most owls and other birds build their nests high in trees or deep in tall grasses, hidden away from predators. Snowy Owls do not hide their nests. Why not? Perhaps because it is difficult to find a hiding place in the wide-open space of the tundra.

A Snowy Owl pair searches for a **nest site** atop one of the highest of the small mounds found on the tundra. These mounds can be from about 8 inches to 3 feet high. Most are found within larger formations called **tundra polygons**. Tundra polygons form as the ground repeatedly melts and refreezes. This causes it to expand and contract, making the surface buckle and form bumps and cracks, just like the ones you see in a roadway.

Scientists think Snowy Owls nest on high spots for several reasons. First, the mounds will be the first places to lose the winter snowpack, and won't be wet and marshy like the rest of the tundra in the spring. The wind atop the mounds helps provide the nesting owls with relief from the many mosquitoes and other biting insects. Also, if the owls can't hide, they must be ready to protect their nestlings. Perched atop a mound or ridge, Ukpik has a good view of approaching danger and is prepared to defend its nest against wolves, bears, foxes, other owls, and even humans!

The Stalking Game! To learn how to play this quiet game, see page 61.

The Incubation Period

Once the owls have mated and chosen a nest site, the female is ready to lay her eggs in mid- to late May. Snowy Owls don't "build" nests, as most birds do. They simply scratch out a small bowl-shaped indentation atop the tundra polygon and the mound is ready. The female Snowy Owl lays her eggs **asynchronously**, which means not at the same time. She usually lays four to eight round, white eggs (about the size of the chicken eggs in your refrigerator), one every two to three days. This means that the oldest chick may hatch up to two weeks sooner than the youngest chick!

Once the eggs are laid, the mother's job is to **incubate** them. That means she has to lie on the nest in the **incubating position**, with her head low and stomach down, keeping the eggs warm all the time. In order to transfer more body heat to the eggs, the mother bird loses some feathers on her chest and belly, making a bare spot called a **brood patch**. Her body covers the eggs like a blanket, keeping them warm and safe beneath her.

It's easy to tell when a pair of Snowies is nesting. The female will be lying down, incubating the eggs, and the male will be **roosting** (sitting up) watching for danger.

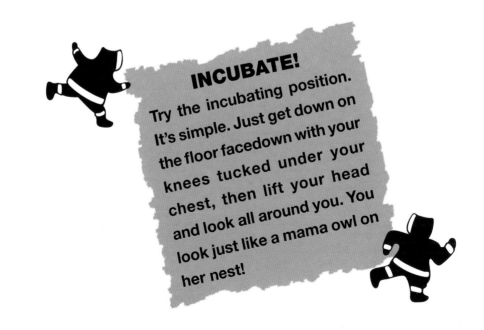

INCUBATE!

Try the incubating position. It's simple. Just get down on the floor facedown with your knees tucked under your chest, then lift your head and look all around you. You look just like a mama owl on her nest!

22

Feeding the Family

Do you like breakfast in bed? During incubation and brooding, female Snowy Owls rarely leave the nest, so it's up to the male to provide food for himself and his mate, plus the chicks once they hatch. Ukpik spends many hours day and night hunting and bringing prey to the nest. The hunt can be divided into three categories: **search**, **pursuit**, and **capture**.

Owls search for their prey from the ground or from atop a perch like a tundra polygon or even a telephone pole. Sometimes they **hover** in one spot in the sky, kind of like jogging in place in midair!

Once it has located its prey, Ukpik may pursue it in several different ways. Commonly, a Snowy Owl will swoop down from its perch and approach prey with hardly a flap of the wings. This can be called either **slipping** or **gliding**. Or the owl may **chase** the prey with fast flight and constant wing beating. Sometimes a hovering owl will **drop** from above onto its prey. And the final pursuit technique is the **run**, in which the Snowy Owl will simply run after its prey on the ground. Picture that!

Once Ukpik has reached its prey, the owl must try to capture it. The most common method of capture is the **wallop**, in which the owl lands directly upon its prey, grabbing it with its talons. Sometimes Ukpik will perform an acrobatic feat called the **sweep**, catching its prey in the talons of one foot while flying low over the tundra.

Even great hunters like the Snowy Owl sometimes **miss** their intended prey, and sometimes they seem to change their minds midhunt and fly back to their perch to wait, which researchers call **no strike**. However, Snowy Owls are such successful hunters that you might see one of their nests surrounded by dead lemmings just waiting to be eaten!

CHARADES!

Grab a few note cards and a pencil. Write each of Ukpik's hunting techniques on a card: **slip**, **glide**, **chase**, **drop**, and **run**. Take turns drawing cards and silently acting out each technique while your friends or classmates guess which one you chose.

Chicks A'Hatching

How long do you think mother birds sit on their nests before the eggs begin to hatch? For Snowy Owls, the **incubation period** is about one month (usually thirty to thirty-three days). How do these tiny birds break out of their shell? Birds don't have teeth like humans do, but baby birds are equipped with a special bump on the front of their beak called an **egg tooth**. The egg tooth is used to crack and break apart the shell so the chick can emerge.

Remember, the eggs were laid asynchronously. The egg that was laid first will be the first to hatch, so it may hatch up to three days before the next one. Every day or so, a new chick, called a **nestling** or **owlet**, will hatch. When nestlings hatch, they are very small—about the size of a tangerine—and are covered with small, soft, white feathers called **down**. Over the next couple of weeks, their eyes will open, their gray feathers will begin to grow in, and they will grow much larger. Due to asynchronous hatching, a Snowy Owl nest may hold all stages of young, from strong, gray-feathered owlets, to tiny, white owlets, to eggs that haven't hatched yet.

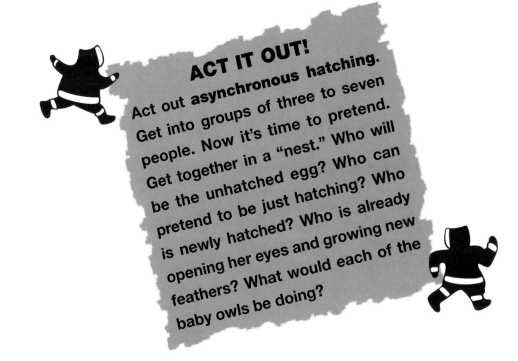

ACT IT OUT!

Act out **asynchronous** hatching. Get into groups of three to seven people. Now it's time to pretend. Get together in a "nest." Who will be the unhatched egg? Who can pretend to be just hatching? Who is newly hatched? Who is already opening her eyes and growing new feathers? What would each of the baby owls be doing?

Brooding the Babies

When a mother bird sits on a nest of unhatched eggs, it is called incubation, right? When she sits on a nest of hatched chicks it is called **brooding**. For the first couple weeks of life Snowy Owlets are helpless; they are unable to see, fly, or **thermoregulate** (maintain their body temperature). Their mother **broods** them by keeping them safely under and around her in the nest.

During this time, the male still does all of the hunting, bringing food back to the nest for his mate. The mother owl then tears apart the meat, giving some to each nestling. If food is abundant, each chick will have plenty to eat. However, if prey is scarce, there may not be enough available to feed all of the nestlings. Sometimes older and larger nestlings receive more food, which can result in starvation of the younger chicks. This allows for the rest of the chicks to receive enough food to grow up strong and healthy.

Nest Defense

Have you ever come between a mother animal and her baby? That is a dangerous place to be. Animal parents protect their young from intruders in many different ways. Some will call out a warning. Others may attack, flee, or try to distract or confuse the intruder. Snowy Owl parents use all of these strategies when defending their nests.

Both the male and the female will call out warnings when they sense danger. Males will **hoot**, females will **scream**, and both will often make a **barking** sound. Most animals would rather give warnings such as these than actually fight another animal. As with a growling dog, you should never approach an animal that is giving you a warning, because if their warning doesn't work, their next step may be to attack.

Many male and some female Snowy Owls have been known to attack intruders and predators approaching their nest. They will usually fly off the nest and dive at intruders with their long legs and sharp talons outstretched until they have driven away the threat. Snowy Owls have been known to attack foxes, dogs, caribou, and even humans that get too close to their young.

NEST DEFENSE!

Okay, actors, who wants to play the predator? Pretend you're an Arctic Fox or other predator sneaking up on the nest. Who wants to be the owl family? Snowy Owl Mom and Dad, how would you defend your kids?

Growing Up Quickly

While Ukpik parents are busy protecting and feeding their chicks, the chicks are busy growing rapidly. During their first week of life, the nestlings triple in weight! An owlet that weighed 40 grams when it hatched would weigh 120 grams at the end of its first week. That's about 4 ounces or ¼ of a pound. Have you ever had a quarter-pound burger? The meat in the burger weighs about as much as a week-old Snowy Owlet. Picture a soft, tiny owl about the size of an apple. It would fit right in the palm of your hand.

In their second week of life Snowy Owl nestlings gain weight even faster. That's also when they begin to change in appearance. Their eyes are slowly opening from small slits to yellow circles by the end of the week. They are transformed from white to gray as their **primary down feathers** are replaced by their **secondary down feathers**. Small, nubby quills called **flight feather sheaths** begin to appear along the edges of their wings. Soon the feathers that allow them to fly will grow from these shafts.

During week three, nestlings are growing their fastest. They weigh over a pound now, and most are losing their egg tooth. By the end of week three, these fluffy gray chicks are beginning to grow their flight feathers but are still far from flying. They are, however, ready to get out and start running around!

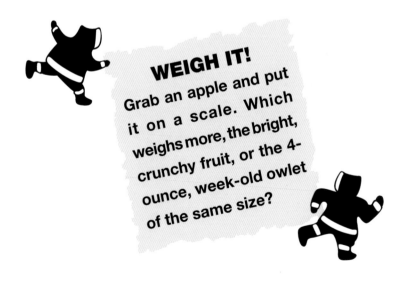

WEIGH IT!
Grab an apple and put it on a scale. Which weighs more, the bright, crunchy fruit, or the 4-ounce, week-old owlet of the same size?

Empty Nest

Can you imagine leaving home as a three-week-old baby? Human babies develop and gain independence more slowly than other animals. At the age of three weeks, Snowy Owlets, though unable to fly, are ready to leave the nest on foot. Scientists call this **nest departure**.

Snowy Owls move into independence more quickly than other large birds of prey. Scientists think that may be an adaptation to their Arctic habitat. Summer in the Arctic is very short. Snowy Owl chicks have only about three months to hatch, grow, disperse, learn to fly, and become independent before the first snows in September. That's a lot to do in such a short time!

When they leave the nest young Snowies still have the downy feathers of nestlings, which don't keep them very warm or dry. Some chicks die in cold weather or rainstorms. They are still unable to fly, so they must be careful of predators. They hide themselves among the grasses and **lichens** (like-ens), mossy plantlike growths that cling to rocks, trees, and tundra. They also stay near their parents, who continue to feed and protect them.

toddling around the tundra

Nest departure sounds dangerous for young owls, but researchers think it might actually keep them safer than staying *in* the nest. Their theory is that if a bear, Arctic Fox, or other predator raids the nest, it will easily eat the entire **clutch** (nest full) of chicks. Once dispersed on the tundra, however, the chicks are well camouflaged and can spread out to hide from predators. Though they are certainly vulnerable to predators at this time, the chances for more of the chicks surviving an attack becomes greater.

Snowy Owlets spend about a month toddling around the tundra near their nest before they fly. Their weight gain has slowed down, but they continue to change appearance rapidly. The **plumage** (feathers) around their eyes and beak is turning lighter, and it's beginning to look like they are wearing a white mask. They are beginning to grow black and white speckled wing **covert** feathers, the small feathers that cover the shafts of their wing feathers, and their flight and tail feathers are growing daily.

By week six, the young begin to look much like adults, though they are still heavily speckled with black, and much of their gray downy plumage remains, especially on their heads. During this time they may look like they're wearing a soft, gray hat!

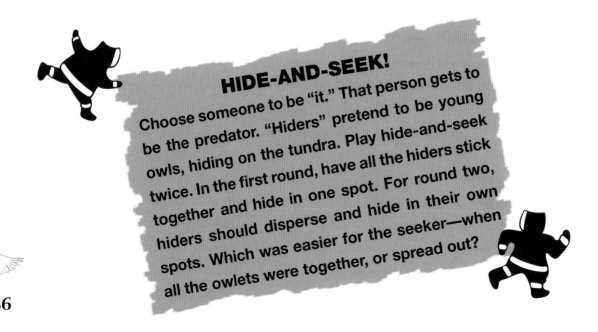

HIDE-AND-SEEK!

Choose someone to be "it." That person gets to be the predator. "Hiders" pretend to be young owls, hiding on the tundra. Play hide-and-seek twice. In the first round, have all the hiders stick together and hide in one spot. For round two, hiders should disperse and hide in their own spots. Which was easier for the seeker—when all the owlets were together, or spread out?

What's a Fledgling?

Have you ever heard the word "**fledgling**"? A fledgling is any baby bird that has left its nest. Once a chick has left the nest, you can say that it has **fledged**. Most songbirds learn to fly within just a few days of fledging. But other birds, like Ukpik, remain flightless for weeks after fledging. It all depends upon how quickly that species grows its **flight feathers**, the feathers on the wing and tail that all birds need to fly.

Two kinds of flight feathers grow on each wing. **Primary feathers** are the very long feathers you see on the tips of a bird's wings, where the "fingers" would be. **Secondary feathers** are shorter flight feathers next to the primaries, running along the back of the wing, or "arm." These feathers work together to give an owl its powerful yet graceful flight.

Now the young owl is ready to fly, right? Not yet! Once its flight feathers are fully grown it still must wait almost a full week for the tail feathers. Why does a bird need tail feathers to fly? you ask. Good question! Without tail feathers, birds would be unable to lift off or steer their flight, much like an airplane without its tail parts. A bird that is unable to steer would end up crashing into something pretty quickly!

Finally Flying!

By the time Snowy Owl fledglings make their first flight, they've already been out of their nest for about three weeks. These almost grown-up birds spend several days hopping around and flapping their wings before "lift-off" occurs. Their first attempts at flight might appear quite comical, but each day of practice finds them staying airborne more and more, starting with just a few feet at a time, and gradually working up to longer distances. Although flying is **innate**, or instinctive, in birds, they still have to practice, just like you did when you were learning to walk.

Most Snowy Owl chicks are six to seven weeks old when they make their first real flight. Have you ever seen a baby bird fly for the first time? Imagine how exciting it would be to see a big Snowy Owl flap its wings and fly off over the tundra for its very first flight!

INSTINCT OR NOT INSTINCT?

List some things that you know how to do by instinct. Then list things that you had to learn and practice. Did you think of a lot of things that take practice? Just like you, young owls spend a lot of time practicing new skills!

40

Autumn Arrives

When you are heading back to school in September, fall has already arrived in the Arctic. Seasons are different in the far north. Alaskan summers are known for their long days and hours of "**midnight sun**." But those summers are short. While snow can fall at any time during the Arctic summer, the first real snow may come to stay in August! By September, days are growing shorter and temperatures are getting colder. It is important that young animals are fully grown and able to take care of themselves by the time winter hits.

How do you stay warm when it's really, really cold and you want to go outside to play? Do you cover your body with layers of warm clothing? That is called **insulating**. When we insulate our bodies or our homes, we cover them with a thick material to keep the heat *in* and cold air and moisture *out*. Many Arctic animals are insulated with warm fur or feathers. Mammals like the Arctic Fox and the Dall Sheep are known for their thick, insulating fur. Snowy Owls have a dense layer of insulating feathers that hold in body heat better than the feathers of almost any other bird. Only the Adélie Penguin of the Antarctic is known to have better insulating plumage than Ukpik!

INSULATING FEATHERS!

How would it feel to be a Snowy Owl? Find a down vest or jacket, put it on, and zip it up. Feel the difference? Warm and cozy in there, isn't it? Down clothes are filled with small down feathers, just like a bird's underfeathers. Now you know how Ukpik stays warm!

Independence

By the time the first snow flies, Snowy Owl chicks are becoming fully independent. Though they may be "hanging around" in family groups, they are spending more time on their own. At age two months, **juvenile** (young) owls are learning to hunt independently. They've spent many weeks on the tundra, watching their parents swoop and chase and gather prey. They are now excellent hunters too. Biologists think that hunting is a skill that an animal learns from its parents, as opposed to an instinctive skill like flying.

At age two months, Snowy Owl youngsters have all of their insulating feathers. They are able to keep themselves warm on those long winter nights. They've practiced their flying skills and are now ready to fly long miles to their **wintering grounds** (the place where they will spend the winter). Researchers aren't sure if they go alone or travel as a family group. Would you rather travel alone or go with your family?

Mysterious Migration

Animals that **migrate** move to different places for different seasons. Most Snowy Owls migrate, leaving their summer breeding grounds to spend their winter farther south. In North America they have a winter range that extends from central Canada across the northern United States. Though Snowies *usually* spend their winters in this region, they have been spotted as far south as Florida!

What scientists don't know are the specific routes and timings of the Snowy Owl migrations, so more research is needed. One way to learn about Snowy Owl migration is to **band** individual owls, where birds are captured, given a small numbered band on one leg, and released. If someone captures the owl again, they can tell by the number on the band where that owl has been before. One owl that was banded in Russia was discovered by scientists in Barrow.

Another way scientists keep track of Snowy Owl locations is through the use of **satellite transmitters**. One of these tiny devices is strapped to the owl's body like a little backpack by biologists who have captured and tranquilized the bird. When the owl is released the transmitter allows humans to chart the location of individual owls through the use of satellites and computers. One owl was charted going from Barrow, Alaska, to Russia, then to Canada, covering thousands of miles on its journey!

Could you ever see a Snowy Owl where you live? Maybe. If your home is in southern Canada or the northern United States, you just might see a wintering Ukpik. Look for them in the habitat they like best: open treeless plains, farmland, or along the coast. Sounds a bit like their Arctic summer home, doesn't it?

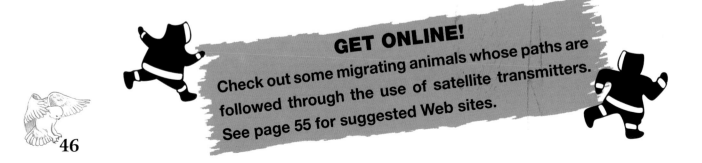

GET ONLINE!
Check out some migrating animals whose paths are followed through the use of satellite transmitters. See page 55 for suggested Web sites.

Facing Danger

How old can a dog live to be? How about a cat? How old do you think Snowy Owls can live to be? The oldest known Snowy in the wild lived to be nine years and five months old. However, one Snowy Owl in captivity lived over twenty-five years!

There are many dangers facing animals in the wild, even for strong predators like Ukpik. Snowy Owls that live near humans are exposed to the most dangers. As with many other animals, collisions with vehicles are one of the leading causes of death for Snowy Owls. Snowy Owls, and many other birds, have also been killed colliding with power lines, airplanes, and other man-made objects.

Just like their chicks, some adult Snowy Owls starve to death when food sources are low. And, sadly, some have been killed deliberately by humans—found shot and abandoned.

Many people are concerned that **global warming** may have a negative impact on the lives of Snowy Owls, as it has on other Arctic animals. Thus far, the effects of a warmer climate on Snowy Owls is unknown.

The Future of Ukpik

What will the future hold for Ukpik? That depends. Just like all wild animals, Snowy Owls need to find enough food, water, shelter, and space to survive and reproduce. Human development is moving into the wilderness in many places where wild animals live. Luckily, many people are working hard to save the habitat Snowy Owls need to survive. In Barrow, Alaska, the native Iñupiat people have set aside large tracts of their land for wildlife conservation to benefit species like Ukpik. In this village, formerly known as Ukpeaġvik, Ukpik has served as a food source, a pet, and an inspiration for adornments, carvings, and even corporate logos. Ukpik has been an important part of the native people's lives for centuries.

Would you like to help secure a place for Snowy Owls in our world? You can help by learning all you can about Ukpik and telling others what you know. When you learn about something, you care about it. And when you care about it, you help protect it. Now that you've learned about Snowy Owls, you can help protect them, too.

LEARN MORE!

Want to learn more about Ukpik? Check out pages 62–63, where you can find books and Web sites with photographs, owl calls, stories, and more.

Do you enjoy learning about animals? Many people who are interested in animals grow up to work with animals. You could be a biologist, an ornithologist, or a veterinarian. Can you think of other jobs where people get to work with animals?

Scientific Names

Scientists like to name things. They especially like to name plants and animals. But unlike most of us, they can't give their favorite critter just any old name. They have to give it a **scientific name**. That way people anywhere in the world will know they are talking about the same plant or animal, even if they use different common names or don't speak the same language. Scientific names are based on Latin or Greek and come in two parts. The first part is the **genus**, and it's always capitalized. Related species have the same genus name. The second part is the **species** name, which is always lowercase. Together, the genus and species make up the scientific name. For example, in the genus *Ursus*, *Ursus maritimus* is the Polar Bear, *Ursus americanus* is the American Black Bear, and *Ursus arctos* is the Brown Bear. Every kind of living thing on earth is supposed to have its own unique scientific name. It doesn't always happen that way, but it's supposed to.

For a long time the Snowy Owl had the scientific name *Nyctea scandiaca*. It was the only owl in the genus *Nyctea*. When they were naming it, scientists thought the Snowy Owl didn't have any close relatives, mostly because it didn't look like other owls. But recently scientists have changed the Snowy Owl's name to *Bubo scandiacus*, putting it in the same genus with the Great Horned Owl. Why the change? Based on studies of DNA (each living thing's unique genetic code) and other physical traits, scientists found that the Snowy Owl is closely related to the other owls in the genus *Bubo*. They now think the reason the Snowy Owl looks so different from its cousins is that it lives in the Arctic. That white plumage and those feathered feet don't mean the Snowy Owl has no close relatives; they just mean it has adapted well to its Arctic home.

Denver Holt and Linda Schueck outfit a Snowy Owl with a satellite transmitter.

Activity

Get Online!
For general information on Snowy Owl migration, see p. 46.

For general information on Snowy Owl migration, see p. 46.

Learn how scientists use satellite tracking to study the movements of birds and animals.

http://magma.nationalgeographic.com/ngm/0212/feature6/index.html
Track Ukpik with the same satellite data used by the researchers around Ukpeaǧvik! You can also find videos, photos, field notes, and links to other sites.

http://www.massaudubon.org/Birds_&_Beyond/snowyowl/index.php
Learn how biologists safely attach satellite transmitters to Snowy Owls.

http://www.massaudubon.org/news/index.php?id=288&type=news
See photographs and read about the satellite tracking of a Snowy Owl in Massachusetts.

http://www.esa.int/esaCP/SEM08MD3M5E_index_0.html
Learn about the satellite tracking of an Eagle Owl and Snowy Owl in Europe.

To see satellite tracking of other birds and animals, check out these sites:

http://www.werc.usgs.gov/sattrack/
Swans, geese, ducks, and more.

http://www.spacetoday.org/Satellites/Tracking/Birds.html
Endangered birds, animals, and fish, from Tundra Swans to caribou to manatees.

http://www.learner.org/jnorth/tm/loon/SatelliteTrackingIndex.html
Common Loons.

Game

Camouflage

Camouflage plays a big role in the food web, which shows the food relationships among plants and animals in an area. As in all food webs, many animals are both predator and prey. Though Snowy Owls are predators, they (especially the young) are also prey to animals like wolves, foxes, and bears. Many animals in the Arctic food web are well camouflaged in their snowy environment. This game demonstrates how animals that may be sneaking up on the Snowy Owlets in the nest will have to use both camouflage and careful movements to get past the mother or father on guard. For more on Snowy Owls and camouflage, see pp. 12–14.

Number of Players: 3 to 30

Play Area: A wooded area outdoors works best, but the game could be adapted to an indoor space as well. An area around 30 by 30 feet (about the size of a classroom) is ideal.

How to play:

1. Set boundaries. Identify any obstacles within the boundaries. If you're playing in the woods, there may be stumps or large rocks that need to be avoided for safety.

2. Choose roles. One person gets to be the Snowy Owl. Ukpik has to stay perched on her mound and can't move her feet. The other players become the camouflaged predators of the tundra (such as wolves, foxes, and bears).

3. The owl closes her eyes and counts to twenty while the predators disperse and hide all around the owl. From her perch the owl opens her eyes and tries to locate as many of the hidden predators as possible. The owl may twist her body to look around, but she may not move her feet. The players who are seen are called out. They get to sit and watch but can't help the owl search.

4. The owl closes her eyes again and counts to ten. All of the predators move closer to the owl, but hide themselves again before the owl opens her eyes. Again, the owl calls out any predators she can see without moving her feet.

5. The owl counts to ten again with each predator moving still closer. This continues until either all predators have been spotted, or a predator gets close enough to tag the owl.

6. If a predator tags the owl, he or she is the winner and the game ends. If all predators are spotted before tagging the owl, the owl wins and the game ends.

Game

Oh, Lemming!

This is an Arctic version of the popular game "Oh, Deer!" It demonstrates how population cycles fluctuate (see p. 18 for information on population cycles). It also shows how all animals need plenty of food, water, and shelter (habitat) to survive.

Number of players: 10 to 30

Play Area: A large outdoor field works best, but a large indoor space, such as a gym, also works.

How to play:

1. Mark two parallel lines about 40 to 60 feet apart.

2. Split your group into two teams. Half the group starts out on one end of the field as lemmings. The other half starts on the other end, with players being the resources animals need to survive: food, water, or shelter. Each team stands on their line with their backs toward the play area.

3. Players who are resources choose which resource to be. Players who choose to be food place their hands on their stomachs. Players who choose to be water place their hands over their mouths. Players who choose to be shelter place their hands over their heads. Each lemming decides what he or she is in need of: food, water, or shelter, and then makes that signal. Once a player has chosen which resource to be/need, he may not change until the next round.

4. A referee calls out, "Oh, Lemming!" and all players turn and face each other. Lemmings then run across the field, still making their symbol, and "take" what they need from the other side. For example, a lemming who is looking for food links arms with a player from the other side who is making the food sign also, and takes that person back to the lemming side to "become" a lemming. Any lemming who was unable to find what he needs to survive "dies" and becomes a resource on the other side. Resources who were not taken stay on the resource side.

5. The next round is played the same as the first, with players choosing a new symbol to make.

6. Rounds can continue to be played as long as needed to demonstrate the population fluctuation of the lemmings. Some rounds they will be very high, other rounds very low, depending on the resources available to them. Classes can keep track of the number of lemmings and resources each round and later plot them on a graph.

7. To make things *really* interesting, choose one or two players to be Snowy Owls. The owls stand on the sidelines, and every once in a while run in to tag a lemming. Lemmings who are tagged are "eaten" and automatically go to the resources side.

Game

The Stalking Game

To learn how Snowy Owl parents pick a nesting site where they can watch out for predators, see p. 20.

This game demonstrates how many predators stalk, or quietly sneak up on, their prey. It also demonstrates how owls have keen senses to locate both prey *and* predators. Much like Camouflage, this game involves other predators (like wolves, foxes, and bears) trying to sneak up on Ukpik, in this case to snatch her eggs.

Number of players: 3 to 30

Play Area: This game works best played outdoors in a large open area, but can be adapted to be played indoors.

How to Play:

1. Choose roles. One player becomes Ukpik. This player is blindfolded and sits in the middle as though dozing on a nest of eggs. The other players become the predators and make a big circle around the owl.

2. Place something noisy, like a bell or a set of keys in front of the owl. This will represent the eggs, which the predators are trying to steal.

3. On a given signal, players begin to sneak slowly and silently toward the owl and her egg. When the owl hears an approaching predator she simply points at the player she hears and that player is out.

4. If a predator is able to steal the egg and make it all the way back to his spot on the circle, that player wins, and the game is over.

5. If all players are heard and pointed out by the owl, the owl wins and the game is over.

Resources

Want to learn more about Snowy Owls? Try these resources:

WEB SITES

www.owlinstitute.org
Learn about the Owl Research Institute in Montana (the place where the idea for this book began!).

http://www.kidsplanet.org/factsheets/snowyowl.html
Learn facts about the Snowy Owl at this great site for kids.

http://www.bbc.co.uk/nature/reallywild/amazing/snowy_owl.shtml
Learn more facts and see beautiful photographs.

http://www.nature.org/initiatives/programs/birds/features/art8959.html
Learn how Harry Potter's owl, Hedwig, is portrayed by male owls in the movies, plus more on the kinds of owls belonging to other characters.

http://www.birds.cornell.edu/AllAboutBirds/BirdGuide/Snowy_Owl.html
Listen to Snowy Owl calls, see range maps, and learn "cool facts."

http://www.audubon.org/bird/cbc/owl_home.html
Find out more about Snowy Owls, plus how you and your family can participate in your local Christmas Bird Count.

http://www.owlpages.com/owls.php?genus=Bubo&species=scandiacus
Listen to a Snowy Owl call here, and find photos, links, and more.

http://www.nwf.org/nationalwildlife/article.cfm?issueID=53&articleID=644
You'll find an informative article here, plus links for more exploration: Line, Les. "Super bird," National Wildlife (February/March 1997), 24–31.

http://library.thinkquest.org/3500/snowy_owl.html
Find information here written by kids for kids.

http://www.mnh.si.edu/ARCTIC/html/owl.html
Learn more about Snowy Owls and other Arctic animals, as well as Native peoples.

KIDS' BOOKS ON SNOWY AND OTHER OWLS

Frost, Helen. *Snowy Owls*. Mankato, MN: Pebble Books, 2006.

Gallop, Louise. *Owl's Secret*. Seattle: Sasquatch Books, 2002.

Gibbons, Gail. *Owls*. New York: Holiday House, 2006.

Hammerslough, Jane. *Owl Puke: Book and Owl Pellet*. New York: Workman Publishing, 2003.

Jarvis, Kila, and Denver W. Holt. *Owls: Whoo Are They?* Missoula, MT: Mountain Press Publishing, 1996.

Mason, Adrienne. *Owls*. Toronto and Tonawanda, NY: Kids Can Press, 2004.

ADULT BOOKS ON OWLS

Berger, Cynthia. *Owls* (Wild Guide). Mechanicsburg, PA: Stackpole Books, 2005.

Duncan, James R. *Owls of the World*. Richmond Hill, ON: Firefly Books, 2003.

König, Claus, et al. *Owls: A Guide to the Owls of the World*. New Haven, CT: Yale University Press, 1999.

Glossary

adaptation. A characteristic that helps give an animal or plant its best chance at survival in the environment where it lives. For example, Snowy Owls have adapted to their Arctic environment by having thick layers of feathers to help keep them warm.

Arctic. The northernmost part of the Earth.

Arctic Circle. An imaginary line around the top part of the Earth, surrounding the North Pole. The area within this line is considered the Arctic.

Arctic tundra. Mostly treeless terrain found very far north.

asynchronous. Not at the same time.

banding. One method of tracking Snowy Owls. Birds are captured by researchers and given a numbered band on one leg. If the same bird is spotted or captured again, researchers can identify it and where it has been, among other things.

bird of prey. A raptor, such as an eagle, hawk, falcon, or owl, that hunts live prey.

breeding ground. The place where an animal raises its young.

brood. To keep nestlings warm, which the parent bird does with its body.

brood patch. The bare skin on a mother bird's chest and belly used to transfer heat from her body to her eggs or chicks.

Brown Lemming. A small mouselike rodent that lives on the tundra. One of the main food sources for Snowy Owls around Barrow, Alaska.

Bubo scandiacus. The scientific name for a Snowy Owl.

camouflage. An adaptation, such as a color or pattern, that allows an animal to blend in visually with its surroundings.

capture. When a Snowy Owl catches its prey.

chase. A hunting method in which Ukpik flies quickly after its prey.

circumpolar. Found around or near the North or South poles.

clutch. A nest full of eggs.

courtship flight. The pattern of flight used mainly by the male Snowly Owl to attract a mate.

covert feathers. Small feathers that cover the bases of larger feathers.

diurnal. Describes animals that are active during the day.

down. The small, soft feathers of a young bird. Also the underfeathers of an adult bird.

drop. A hunting method in which Ukpik drops directly onto its prey.

egg tooth. The small temporary bump on the beak of a baby bird, used to break out of the egg.

fledge. To leave the nest.

fledgling. A young bird that has left the nest and is learning to live independently.

flight feathers. The large feathers on a bird's wings and tail that are needed to fly.

flight feather sheaths. Nubby quills that will grow into flight feathers.

fluctuate. To rise or fall in cycles. For example, the population of Brown Lemmings can fluctuate greatly.

genus. In scientific classification, a group containing one or more species.

glide. A hunting method in which Ukpik glides off its perch to pursue prey.

global warming. A gradual warming of the Earth; also called climate change.

hoot. A call given mostly by male Snowy Owls.

hover. To stay in one place in the air while flying.

incubate. To keep eggs warm before hatching.

incubating position. The way a mother bird lies horizontally with her chest and belly over her eggs.

innate. Inborn; a trait one is born with.

Iñupiaq. The language spoken by the Iñupiat people.

Iñupiat. A group of people native to the Arctic region of Alaska.

insulate. To keep warm by keeping cold out and warmth in.

juvenile. Young.

lichen. A mossy plantlike growth that clings to rocks, trees, and the ground.

midnight sun. A term used to describe the long hours of summer daylight in the Arctic.

migrate. To move to another place seasonally.

miss. When a hunting owl is unable to catch its intended prey.

nest departure. When young owls leave the nest.

nesting. The act of finding a mate, choosing a nest site, and raising a family.

nestling. A young chick, still in the nest.

nocturnal. Describes animals that are active at night.

no-strike. When a Snowy Owl is unable to catch its intended prey.

owlet. A baby owl.

plumage. A bird's set of feathers.

predator. An animal that hunts live creatures for food.

prey. An animal hunted for food by other animals.

primary down feathers. The first set of feathers a young bird grows. These are soft and white on Snowy Owlets.

primary feathers. The longest feathers on the end of a bird's wing, where the hand and fingers would be; also called primaries.

pursuit. The stage of the hunt where a Snowy Owl chases its intended prey.

raptor. A hawk, eagle, falcon, osprey, or owl; bird of prey.

roost. To perch sitting upright.

run. A hunting technique in which Ukpik runs after its prey on the ground.

satellite transmitter. A small transmitter which, when attached to an animal's body, can track its location by bouncing a signal off satellites in space.

scream. A warning call used mostly by female Snowy Owls.

search. When Ukpik is looking for prey to hunt.

secondary down feathers. The second set of down feathers grown by young Snowy Owl chicks. These are soft and gray.

secondary feathers. The second largest set of feathers on a bird's wing, along the forearm; also called secondaries.

slip. A hunting method in which Ukpik slips from its perch to catch its prey.

species. In scientific classification, a group of closely related living things; Snowy Owls are a species of owl. One or more species make up a genus.

sweep. A hunting method in which Ukpik catches its prey in the talons of one foot while flying low over the tundra.

talons. The sharp claws on a raptor's feet.

thermoregulate. The ability to control one's body temperature.

tundra polygon. Mounds or small hills created by the cycle of freezing and thawing on the Arctic tundra.

Ukpeaġvik. The Iñupiaq name for Barrow, Alaska, meaning "Place where Snowy Owls are hunted."

Ukpik. The Iñupiaq name for the Snowy Owl.

undulate. To move in a wavelike motion, as in the courtship flight of the Snowy Owl.

wallop. A hunting method in which a Snowy Owl lands directly upon its prey, grabbing it in its talons.

wingspan. The distance from wingtip to wingtip when a bird's wings are outstretched.

wintering ground. The place where an animal spends the winter months.

Index

Ansley Watson Ford is an elementary-school teacher and cochairs the education committee of the Flathead Audubon Society in Western Montana. *Snowy Owls* is her first book.

Denver W. Holt is the founder and president of the Owl Research Institute in Charlo, Montana. In addition to the many scientific papers he has written, he is the coauthor of *Owls: Whoo Are They?*, also available from Mountain Press.

Jennifer White Bohman holds a bachelor's degree in fine arts from the University of Montana. She discovered her interest in birds of prey while volunteering at the Owl Research Institute.